A Word of Encouragement to Young Converts

By Ernest S. Williams

Gospel Publishing House
Springfield, Mo., U. S. A.

A WORD OF ENCOURAGEMENT

You have now accepted Christ as your Saviour and given your heart to Him, and it is your earnest desire to do His will. A few kindly words of advice will help you on your way.

There are three things essential to your success—prayer, reading the Bible, and faith. In prayer your heart is speaking to God, and in prayer you will learn that God responds and quickens you. Reading the Bible is like eating your food, it makes you strong. It also teaches you to understand God and His will for you. Faith is simple trust in the promises of the Bible and in the power and love of God. We will now mention a few things to help you, to which you will do well to give serious consideration.

ASSURANCE

Assurance is that impression which came to your heart upon your accepting Jesus as your Saviour, by which you felt certain that you were received by Him. This assurance must be cultivated, for, as you live for God, Satan will tempt you and may try to make you doubt even that you are saved. The tempter has been likened to a ravenous fowl which would try to take out of your heart the good seed of salvation and the Word of God. Matt. 13:19. Do not be surprised when he comes, and do not doubt. "Cast not away therefore your confidence, which hath great recompense of reward." Heb. 10:35. You know you are saved because Jesus died for you upon the cross and bore all your sins, and not altogether by the way you may at times feel.

You were not saved by feeling but by faith, Eph. 2:8. Neither are you kept by feeling but by faith. "Kept by the power of God through faith," 1 Peter 1:5. Feelings come and go and rise and fall like the tide and waves of the sea. James 1:5. Your anchor must grip the unchanging Rock, Christ Jesus. Your salvation in the first place and your continued safety in Him depends upon the unchangeableness of His love (lo, I have loved thee with an everlasting love, Jer. 31:3) and of His word (Forever, O Lord, Thy word is settled in heaven, Psa. 119:89). So, you see, as you abide, you are forever safe, regardless of your feelings.

Here are some more promises on which you may ever rely, knowing that as you trust in them, you are saved and safe. "Him that cometh to me I will in no wise cast out." John 6:37. You have come to Him, and He has accepted you. Do you then think He would cast you out or turn His back upon you when the hour of temptation comes? Oh, no, for He has said, "I will never leave thee nor forsake thee." Heb. 13:5.

He who has saved you has promised to keep you, so you must always trust in Him and never in yourself. You have now become one of those "who are kept by the power of God, through faith, unto salvation ready to be revealed in the last time." 1 Pet. 1:5. You see, it is God who saved you, and it is He who will keep you. "He which hath begun a good work in you will perform it until the day of Jesus Christ." Phil. 1:6. All through life, wherever you may go or whatever your circumstances may be, the Lord will ever be with you. The following Scripture verses will greatly help you if you keep them in your heart.

Assurance is the fruit of faith. Eph. 3:12; 2 Tim. 1:12; Heb. 10:22. Of what are we assured? (a) Eternal life. 1 John 5:13; (b) The abiding love of God. Rom. 8:38, 39; (c) Our union with Christ. Eph. 5:30; 1 John 4:13; (d) Peace with God. Rom. 5:1; (e) Continuance in grace. Phil. 1:6; (f) Heaven. John 14:1-3.

DEVOTIONAL LIFE

We have mentioned in the beginning that those who take our Lord Jesus as their personal Saviour should cultivate definite times of prayer. This is very important. In the first place we always need the Lord so much. Then, too, God has saved us that communion with Him might be restored. Prayer is communion with God. Communion means sharing. In prayer we share with God our worship, thanksgiving, and praise, and we tell Him of our trials and needs. He then shares with us His love and fellowship, and, hearing our prayers, He helps us in our trials and meets our needs. Different persons have tried to describe prayer. "Prayer is the voice of faith." *Horne.* "Prayer is an offering up of our desires to God, for things agreeable to His will, in the name of Christ, with confession of our sins and thankful acknowledgment of His mercies." *Westminster Catechism.* "A prayer, in its simplest definition, is merely a wish turned heavenward." *Phillips Brooks.* Prayer is your heart talking to God.

Your life ought to be so planned that you may have definite times each day in which to wait on God in Prayer. Daniel prayed three times each day. Dan. 6:10. David said, "Evening, and morning, and at noon, will I pray." Psalm 55:17. You may not always have opportunity to run away to a place of quiet at the noon hour, but your heart can pray, and you can arrange to have some time definitely set apart each day in which to wait on God. Be not in a hurry when you pray. Take time to wait with praise and gratitude before the Lord. He may wish to speak to you as well as to have you speak to Him, letting you know what His will for you is for the day. Cultivate looking to

Him for guidance. You are now His child and He has promised to lead and instruct you. As you learn to wait on Him you will find your spiritual life enriched and deepened in the knowledge of Him.

Now we wish you to study the Scriptures given below that you might learn how others have waited on God and prayed.

Prayer is an evidence of conversion. Acts 9:11.

Nothing should hinder our lives of prayer. Dan. 6:10.

How shall we pray? (a) Seek God, Psalm 34:4, with all the heart. Jer. 29:12, 13; (b) Wait upon God. Psalm 40:1; (c) Ask in faith. James 5:15; (d) According to God's will. 1 John 5:14; (e) In the name of Christ. John 14:13.

Examples of prayer: Gen. 24:12; 32:9-12; 1 Sam. 1:10; 2 Kings 20:2; Dan. 9:3, 17; Acts 4:23-31; 9:40; 10:30; 12:5-7.

BAPTISM

As soon after accepting Jesus as your personal Saviour as possible you ought to be baptized in water in obedience to the commandment of Jesus. Matt. 28:19. The correct method of baptism is by immersion; that is, by being put entirely under the water as this method alone fulfills a "burial," and in baptism we signify that we are "buried with Christ by baptism into death." Rom. 6:4. And what does this death mean? It means the giving up of everything that one knows of that might not be pleasing to God, for sin is doing that which God does not approve. Coming up out of the waters of baptism, one is then to "walk in newness of life," or in the new life which one has received from God. This new life is spiritual in contrast to the old life, or the life which one lived before one was saved, which was carnal.

When contemplating baptism one ought to examine oneself and put one's all into the hands of God in full surrender to His will. This may perhaps be summed up by saying one ought to surrender one's will to the will of God, for if God has one's will, He will have His way in one's life. As you live the Christian life, you will learn that the all important secret of successful Christian living is in being able always to say as Jesus did, "Not my will, but thine be done." In baptism you acknowledge that you are not your own, but that you entirely belong to the Lord and wish to be His love servant to go where He might wish you to go, to serve in any way that He might direct, and, if need be to suffer for Him with an entire submissiveness to His will.

Some believe one ought to be buried three times in baptism, once in the name of the Father, then in the name of the

Son, then in the name of the Holy Ghost. We believe you can readily see that these sincere people are not correct when you consider that in baptism one signifies that one is buried by baptism into the death of Christ, and since Jesus died only once, of course one ought to be baptized only one time, or by what we call single immersion.

You may read the following Scriptures on baptism.

Jesus was baptized. Matt. 3:13-15.

Jesus commanded that we be baptized. Matt. 28:19.

Baptism is to be administered in the name of the Father, and of the Son, and of the Holy Ghost. Matt. 28:19.

Baptism signifies a burial with Christ. Rom. 6:4.

We are to be baptized in faith. Acts 8:36, 37.

BE FILLED WITH THE SPIRIT

After receiving Jesus as your Saviour and Lord, and having been baptized in water as He has commanded you, you ought to open your heart to receive the baptism with the Holy Spirit. This is an enduement of spiritual power which will enable you to live better for Him. The disciples were saved before Pentecost, but they had not this baptism. Those at Samaria also gave every evidence of having found Jesus as their Saviour, for upon accepting the preaching of Philip "there was great joy in that city"; also the converts were baptized in water, which Philip would not have granted them had they not chosen Jesus as their Saviour and Lord. But when Peter and John came down, they laid their hands upon them and prayed for them that they might be filled with the Spirit "for as yet He was fallen upon none of them." Acts 8:16.

During the latter part of the ministry of Jesus, He spoke often to His disciples of the Spirit whom they should receive. John 14:16. Then after His resurrection He commanded them "that they should not depart from Jerusalem, but wait for the promise of the Father," Acts 1:4, explaining that "ye shall receive power after that the Holy Ghost is come upon you." Acts 1:8. It was at Pentecost that the promise of Jesus was fulfilled, and upon being filled with the Spirit, all the disciples "began to speak with other tongues as the Spirit gave them utterance." Acts 2:4. This same manifestation from God also accompanied the baptism with the Spirit throughout apostolic times, and we believe God wishes all to be so yielded to Him and so filled with the Spirit that the same sign will follow the same baptism today. You should therefore begin to tarry now in earnest surrender and faith for this infilling with the Spirit if you have not yet received.

Read the following Scriptures about this.

The baptism with the Spirit comes from Christ. Matt. 3:11.

It is promised to those who believe. Acts 1:5; 2:28, 39; 11:16; John 14:16, 17; 15:26; 16:7-15.

It is to be earnestly sought. Luke 11:13; Acts 1:4, 5, 14; 5:32.

How is it received? Acts 2:1-4; 8:14-17; 10:44-48; 19:2-7.

A CHURCH HOME

You will perhaps want to make the place where you were saved your church home. It is well, if possible, to become united with a well organized church, preferably one that has a constitution and by-laws by which it conducts its business. Healthy church environments are as necessary for the healthy growth of a Christian as are health-producing home surroundings for the healthy growth of a babe. Although some children grow up into healthy strong men who have not had proper surroundings in their earlier days, and it is possible for one to mature into a strong Christian even where spiritual surroundings are not the best, unfortunately, there are many who weaken and die.

When you have become a member of a church, attend the services as regularly as possible. "Not forsaking the assembling of ourselves together." Heb. 10:25. Take an active part in testimony as opportunity affords, for "with the heart man believeth unto righteousness, and with the mouth confession is made unto salvation." Rom. 10:10. Testimony is a great help to the one who gives it, and it also makes one a blessing to others. Philem. 6. Then be sure to take an active part in the prayer meetings, street meetings, or other means of service, and show lively interest in winning others to Christ. As you keep busy about your Father's business, you will grow in grace and become a joy to your pastor and a blessing to many.

Consult your pastor concerning Christian work, and he will doubtless be able to direct you to the line of activity in the Lord's work to which you are especially suited.

Remember also that since you are now a child of God, the work of God, through the channels of the church, ought to receive at least one-tenth of your income, as the tithe of what one earns belongs to the Lord. Your conscience must tell you just how this money should be distributed. Of course, the pastor ought to have support, needed things connected with carrying on the work of the church should be helped, and there ought to be some portion of your giving which would go regularly for foreign missions, since missions is the plan of God, who has said,

"Go ye into all the world and preach the gospel to every creature."

The church (a) Belongs to God. 1 Tim. 3:5; (b) Is built on Christ. 1 Cor. 3:11; (c) Is the body of Christ. Eph. 1:23; (d) Is loved by Christ. Eph. 5:25; (e) Is purchased by Christ. Acts 20:28; (f) Is added to. Acts 2:47; 5:14; (g) Is not to be neglected. Heb. 10:24, 25; 1 Cor. 16:2; 2 Cor. 9:7; Luke 11:42.

LIVING FOR GOD

God has saved us that we might serve Him. This service is to be the fruit, not of fear, but of love. "Fear hath torment. He that feareth is not made perfect in love." 1 John 4:18. There is a fear of reverence, a holy awe, an earnest desire that we may not grieve the Spirit; but fear with a dread in it ought to be ever resisted if we are walking in the light.

Living for God is a walk in holiness, a putting off of all things that are condemned, and a putting on of those things which please the Lord. It is always a walk of faith for "without faith it is impossible to please Him." Heb. 11:6. Evil thoughts and evil feelings must be refused and put away from our hearts, such as anger, evil speaking, and other unkind or unholy things. It is not a sin of our heart if these things present themselves to us and we overcome them by refusing to receive them. Sin comes only when we welcome evil into our lives.

In living for God, be always honest and careful. Avoid, if at all possible, going into debt. It is much easier to keep out of debt than to pay debts. A reputation for honesty is one of the greatest assets which a Christian can have. Give honest employment. A Christian ought to be as faithful to his duties when alone as when his employer is standing over him. Both God and the world are looking for persons whom they can trust.

Be truthful. Some find it easy to tell "little lies." Remember a lie ruined our first parents, and a lie may ruin us. Moreover, "all liars shall have their part in the lake that burneth with fire and brimstone." Rev. 21:8.

Live for God everywhere. It might become a temptation to some, should they be among certain company or in places where their Christian friends might not see them, to let down in their mode of living. In such compromise there is great danger. Always live as "unto the Lord and not unto men" with the consciousness that whoever else may or may not see you, the Scripture is always true, "Thou God seest me." Since we belong to Him, it is He before whom we are always to walk.

Walk in love. Eph. 5:2; 1 John 4:11, 12, 17, 18.

Put off the old man. Eph. 4:22; Rom. 6:6, 11, 14.

Put on the new man. Eph. 4:24.

Lie not. Eph. 4:25; Rev. 21:8.

Owe no man. Rom. 13:8.

LOOKING LIKE CHRIST

There is a beautiful Scripture found in 2 Cor. 3:18 which says, "But we all, with open face beholding as in a glass the glory of the Lord, are changed into the same image from glory to glory, even as by the Spirit of the Lord." This shows that if we walk in the Spirit and live in thankfulness, praise and victory, the glory of the Lord will so fill us that it will be seen to radiate through us. When Moses came down from the mount, "he wist not that the skin of his face shone." Exod. 34:29. The glory of God had covered his countenance, but he was not aware of it. And when Stephen stood before his accusers they "saw his face as it had been the face of an angel." Acts 6:15.

You are now one of those which are to shine for Jesus, radiant with the glory of God, one of those privileged ones which are to "adorn the doctrine of God our Saviour in all things." Tit. 2:10. This means that you should shun as companions those who do not love the Lord and that you should "love not the world, neither the things that are in the world" (1 John 2:15); that you should refrain

from going to places which your heart
and conscience tell you Jesus would not
have you to go.

The way you dress is also included.
The Bible is plain concerning one's apparel. "Whose adorning let it not be
that outward adorning of plaiting the
hair, and of wearing of gold, or of putting on of apparel; but let it be the hid-
den man of the heart . . . the ornament
of a meek and quiet spirit which is in the
sight of God of great price." 1 Pet. 3:3,
4. No set rules can be laid down as to
just how young people ought to dress,
since fashions are continually changing,
and it is not necessary that one to be a
Christian must look always "years out
of date." But there are some general
rules which a Christian ought always to
follow. One's dress ought always to be
modest. Ask yourself, "Is this modest?
Will the wearing of it glorify God?" If
you feel it does not meet these require-
ments, do not wear it no matter how
many others may do so. Be not afraid
to be looked upon as different from others, for you surely are. You are a
Christian.

Love not the world. 1 John 2:15-17.

Whose adorning. 1 Tim. 2:9; 1 Pet.
3:3, 4.

Make no compromise. 2 Cor. 6:14 to
7:1.

STUDY YOUR BIBLE

It is always well for a Christain to read of the lives of good men and to read good books written by godly people. Trashy reading, such as cheap novels, ought always to be avoided. Concerning what you read, always ask yourself, "Will reading this tend to make me a better or more useful person, or will it fill my mind with trash?" Our minds are a great workshop. We can fill them with useful things or with wasteful litter.

The greatest of all books to read is the Bible because it is God's Word, inspired by the Holy Spirit, and therefore the choicest of all literature. Have you ever seen a little boy and heard his mother calling him, while he was too much filled with play to hear her voice? That is the way some people read the Bible. They read the words, but their minds are really taken up with something else. Such readers receive little help from their reading. We should practice trying to shut out all other thought and, in that state, to thoughtfully read the Scriptures. Then we should meditate upon what we have read to get the meaning, as in this way we learn the will of the Lord for us. In reading the Word, one is taught about God. salvation, peace, holiness, and eternal life, and one learns how to resist temptation, to understand God's dealings with one, and to obtain things promised.

In fact, through reading the Scriptures, one is taught how to intelligently serve God and to appropriate the blessings of His kingdom to one's heart. Because of lack of understanding of the Scriptures, some Christians lead a rather aimless Christian life, living alone on such passing blessings as chance to come to them. Through study and meditation, we learn the richness of Christian grace, which is so much more than just a passing happy feeling. Driving one day through Virginia, where different battles of the Civil War had been fought, I saw in place after place signs telling about the battle that had been fought there. In reading God's Word we learn of many battle fields and of many spiritual victories which others have won. Becoming familiar with these victories they won will greatly help us in our trials and in our battles. Through learning of the tests and victories of others, we will learn something of the reasons why we must pass through some of the experiences which will be ours. Read the Bible every day, for in it is found the Bread of life, strength of God for your soul.

The Scriptures inspired of God. 2 Tim. 3:16.

Believed in and taught by Christ. Matt. 4:4; Mark 12:10; John 7:42; Luke 24:27.

Are full and sufficient. Luke 16:29, 31.

Benefits of (a) Producing faith. John

20:31; Rom. 10:17; 15:4; (b) Cleansing of the heart. John 15:3; Eph. 5:26; (c) Building up. 1 Pet. 2:2; Acts 20:32.

TEMPTATION

You will be tempted, but temptation in itself is not sin, for man was tempted before sin ever entered into the world, and Jesus the holy Son of God, was tempted in all points like as we are. Instead of temptation causing God to be displeased with us, we learn from Him that "blessed is the man that endureth temptation, for when he is tried, he shall receive the crown of life, which the Lord hath promised to them that love Him." James 1:12.

The different ways in which one may be tempted are so many that they have been spoken of as "divers temptations," (James 1:2) and "manifold temptations." 1 Pet. 1:6. If you will trust the Lord through the trial when you are tempted and "resist (the devil) steadfast in the faith," (1 Peter 5:9) you will come forth from the trying hour after the example of Jesus, who "returned from the wilderness in the power of the Spirit." Luke 4:14.

God allows us to be tempted that the quality of our character and the sincerity of our consecration may be proved; Satan tempts us, wishing to induce us to do something evil. Although we are saved, we are yet in the body, and there are certain natural characteristics of the natural man which Satan would like to debase. These characteristics have been spoken of as one's "own lusts," and in the temptation one is said to be "drawn away and enticed" of them. James 1:14. Now these "lusts" are any desires which Satan may seek to induce us to yield to in any way that would lead us away from God and righteousness. We must therefore be alert, not only to resist temptations to wicked things as we usually understand them, but also to detect Satan when he may come as an angel of light to deceive us by the temptation, seeking to cause us to believe that we may obtain further knowledge of God without the necessity of making sacrifices which Christians are ordinarily required to make. 2 Cor. 11:14.

Temptation to evil comes from Satan. James 1:13; Matt. 4:1.

Instruments that may be used: (a) Personal lusts. James 1:14. (b) Covetousness. 1 Tim. 6:9, 10. (c) Evil associates. Prov. 1:10.

Temptation is permitted as a trial of faith. 1 Pet. 1:7. And patience. James 1:2, 4.

God enables one to bear. 1 Cor. 10:13.

Victory comes through faith in Christ. 1 John 5:4, 5.

Blessedness of those who overcome. James 1:2-4, 12.

SHOULD YOU SIN

"Whatsoever is born of God overcometh the world." 1 John 5:4. "We know that whosoever is born of God sinneth not; but he that is begotten of God keepeth himself, and that wicked one toucheth him not." 1 John 5:18. These verses show how definitely we may always be kept in victory. You should never, therefore, look for defeat.

But should you sin, what ought you to do? John knew that one might become snared by the tempter, so wrote, "And if any man sin, we have an advocate with the Father, Jesus Christ the righteous." 1 John 2:1. You see, then, that while Jesus wishes to keep us from sinning, at the same time if we should be overcome, He does not desert us, but, instead, acts as our lawyer before the justice of God. And what does He plead in our behalf? The wounds which He bore at Calvary. He shows the Father how He bore the penalty of our sins and how, through the shedding of His blood in our behalf, as long as our hearts desire to love and serve Him, we may be forgiven even should it be necessary again and again.

Should you at any time become conscious of having done something that has grieved the heart of the Lord; should you sin with your tongue or omit doing something which you ought to do; should you become conscious of pride, of impatience, of covetousness, or of failing to witness; or should you feel that you were losing your first love or were growing lukewarm, remember that Jesus is always at the right hand of the Father making intercession for you and "if we confess our sins, He is faithful and just to forgive us our sins and to cleanse us from all unrighteousness." 1 John 1:9. The tempter may at such a time tempt you to discouragement, to feel "what is the use?" or to "throw the whole thing up!" Remember that any such thoughts come, not from the Lord, and not from your own self alone, but from Satan, and surely you are not going to submit to him, are you?

Letting you know it is possible for one to sin, and telling you of the Saviour's love for us even then, does not mean that we expect you to sin. By no means. We are expecting you to continue to grow in grace and in the knowledge of our Lord and Saviour. To have always a happy victorious life, learn to live in continuous dependence on Christ, to trust the continuous cleansing of His blood, and with your heart to say, "Lord, I take Thee to be my life, my wisdom, my righteousness, and my strength." He will prove Himself to be a guide, a comforter, a friend, and a keeper.

God forgives His people. Psalm 130:3, 4, 7; 1 John 1:9; 2:1, 2.

Jesus is our great High Priest. Heb. 4:14-16; 7:26; 9:24.

We are to look to Jesus and praise Him. Heb. 12:2; 13:15.

AIM AT PERFECTION

Jesus has said, "Be ye therefore perfect even as your Father which is in heaven is perfect." Perfection, therefore, ought to be the goal to which all Christians seek to come. Be not discouraged if you do not arrive at perfection all at once. There is first the blade, then the ear, and after that the full corn in the ear. Mark 4:28. To become perfect in the sense of coming "unto the measure of the stature of the fullness of Christ," (Eph. 4:13) requires time, testing, temptation, and trust. One's heart may be perfect from the moment one is saved in that one loves God supremely and wishes to live only for Him. It is development in perfection that requires years of yielding and learning from the Lord. This includes many lessons, trials, and experiences, during which one must learn always to say "not my will, but thine be done." When one is first saved, one is but an infant in the family of God. 1 Pet. 2:2. From this, one grows into childhood, then youth, and, finally, into ripened experience. 1 John 2:12-14.

God as a faithful and holy Father will chasten you, test you, and allow your faith to be tried. Heb. 12:6. Sometimes you will not understand why you have to pass through such severe testing and at times you will not be able to see the way before you. Then, like Job, you must learn to say, "But He knoweth the way that I take; when He hath tried me, I shall come forth as gold." Job 23:10. Have faith in God. Remember you are God's child and nothing can separate you from His love. Rom. 8:38, 39. Have faith in Him no matter what the trial may be. He is refining the gold, separating the dross which you cannot see, washing your garments, and ironing out the wrinkles so that you may be presented with His glorious church, "not having spot, or wrinkle, or any such thing, but that it should be holy and without blemish." Eph. 5:27.

God bless you as you journey toward the Holy City. The way will lead sometimes by quiet waters (Psa. 23:2); sometimes over stormy seas (Mark 4:38); sometimes by way of waters of blessing to swim in (Ezek. 47:5); and at other times by way of the waterless desert (Deut. 8:2). Whatever may be the way, Jesus will always be with you, so never fear.

Paul sought perfection. Phil 3:12. Perfection of love is perfection of heart. Col. 3:14. Perfect Christlikeness is perfection of development. Eph. 4:12, 13. Patience leads to perfection. James 1:4.

SOME FURTHER SUGGESTIONS

You will find it an excellent thing to subscribe for a good spiritual paper. You will receive much help in your spiritual life through the *Pentecostal Evangel.* This paper is published weekly, and is *$1.00 per year;* Canadian and foreign *$1.50 per year.*

The *Christ's Ambassadors Herald* is a 16-page monthly magazine appreciated by any reader, but especially enjoyed by young folk. *Price, 5c per copy; 60c per year; two years $1.00.*

Do you wish to study the Bible? Our *Systematic Bible Study Courses* will be found most helpful. There are 14 textbooks comprising the Elementary, Standard, and Advanced Courses. The 12 books of Elementary and Standard Courses may be had at 50c each. Free certificates are awarded for satisfactory work on any one of the 14 textbooks. If interested, you may send for free descriptive folder.—GOSPEL PUBLISHING HOUSE, Springfield, Mo.